IT'S HARD TO FIND GOOD HELP THESE DAYS
A CUSTOMER SERVICE MANUAL FOR BUSINESSES

By

Jeanne "Bean" Murdock

Library of Congress Control Number 2014907078
ISBN 0-9770678-7-4
EAN 978-0-9770678-7-9
The information, recommendations, instructions,
and advice contained in this book are intended for
general reference purposes.

This book was initially registered with
the copyright office in 2012.

Cover image by Julie Lopez with model
Maurica Anderson.

I dedicate this book to professionals who provide customer service beyond the expected level, knowing that they won't receive a tip.

ACKNOWLEDGMENTS

Thanks to David Henley for reading my manuscript and giving me the confidence to move forward with this very needed project. His kind words mean a lot, considering his success as an author and reporter.

TABLE OF CONTENTS

Foreword

FOREWORD

Last July, while doing business at the California Mid-State Fair in Paso Robles, a couple of my long-time friends approached me and started our customary once-a-year friendship renewal. Something they said still sticks in my mind, prompting me to continue improving myself: "When we see Geary Whiting, we know things are going to be alright." People who receive that compliment have done something special with their life. I can't help but think of the saying, "Lord, help me become the person my dog thinks I am." Perhaps I am finally arriving.

When asked to write this foreword, I felt honored; perhaps I have become the person my dog thinks I am.

As the saying goes, "You can't teach an old dog new tricks." WRONG! This old dog, who obtains respected credentials, has been around the block a few times, runs a successful business, and makes a nice difference in people's lives, does learn new tricks. Upon reading parts of Jeanne's book, which you now hold in your hand, I have either learned something new, or at least I have been lovingly reminded of important things that I had forgotten.

Jeanne "Bean" Murdock does a wonderful job presenting valuable information for our benefit. Her straight-forward, practical approach is very refreshing in our degenerated, "politically correct" society. She is honest and CLEAR! This book is for those who want more out of life, not those who are being entertained by TV, movies, and parties. This book is character building.

I first met Jeanne when I was having coffee with some of my special friends whose conversation that day was on the subject of "elegance, and how does one define it?" This topic had been on my mind for some time, because I rarely see this exceptional quality in a man or woman. When a warm voice asked, "Is that your vehicle outside?" I looked up and there stood our subject: "Elegance." That was the beginning of a wonderful friendship.

Out of future conversations with Jeanne came respect and admiration. She is not only an elegant, ambitious woman, but also smart.

I feel you will enjoy reading this book. So grab a warm cup of coffee, or perhaps a glass of your favorite wine, and sit, read, think and learn, or re-learn, and let Jeanne grow on you.

I will conclude this rather lengthy foreword by sharing one of my favorite sayings:

GREAT MINDS talk about dreams. AVERAGE MINDS talk about events. LITTLE MINDS talk about people.
---Eleanor Roosevelt

Jeanne "Bean" Murdock...Dares to Dream :)

---Geary Whiting

INTRODUCTION

What was your worst experience with a customer? What was the outcome? What was your best experience with a customer? What was the outcome? People have expectations of how they will be treated when they hire professionals, whether via investing in a service or product. When their expectations aren't met, they tend to feel like they are not getting their money's worth or that they are "wronged".

For any one person, customer service expectations may vary from store to store. "At store A I'm going to be treated like a queen. I love it. At store B I'll be treated like a number. I'm used to it." Similarly, expectations vary from person to person. Some people want their hand held through the whole process, while others prefer feeling independent. Since you don't know what people, especially new customers, expect unless they tell you, you should practice the highest level of service at all times. Of course. Equally important is listening.

Many times in this book, listening will be referenced along with "Shhh! Listen!" How can you help customers if you don't know what they want? How do you know what they want if you're not listening? Shhh! Stop talking! People offer you the keys to effective customer service when you listen. Listen! They'll tell you how to please them.

I want to teach you how to read body language, also, but although I practice reading body language, teaching it is not my area of expertise. Reading body language, including facial expressions, is another form of communication that informs you of what customers want. But if you misread them, it could be disastrous. For now, just read this book and ask customers, "How can I help you?"

My passion for excellent customer service developed early in life, watching my parents demand great treatment. Both having a background in the hospitality industry, they knew how to take good care of customers, which matched how they wanted to be treated. My parents always vocalized their content and discontent with professionals. They gave plenty of praise when deserved as well as suggestions where there was room for improvement.

As early as my late teens, I started writing letters to companies when I was severely disappointed about how I was treated. In those cases, I always left a store whispering under my breath, "I'm going to write a letter."

It wasn't until my late thirties that I realized my letter writing started in elementary school. My mom came across some of my school papers, including a letter I had to write to a fictitious company for a class assignment. Apparently, I was instructed to write a letter based on my frustration with a store. This is the original letter:

To the Fish Manager
Finnigans Pet Fish St.
San Jose, Calif.
Calif. 12

Joanne Murdoch
125 Yorkshire St.
Cupertino, Ca.
Jan. 11, 1978

Dear Mr. H. S. Glide:

I am writing you to complain about the fish!

The dumb fish are bothering mine. I bought it from the pet shop. He assured me it wouldn't bite would eat dried food unlike the rest of the fish...

... fish ...

... If you don't do something about it I will go to the pet store...

... Thank you for your time

In case you couldn't read the letter:

Dear Mr. H.J. Ghoti:

I am demanding you to do something about your fish!

The dumb fish are bothering mine! I bought it from Tommy McGee. He assured me it was harmless. It would eat dry fish food like the rest of the fish in your tank. The fish has eaten all of my collection. He has eaten $100 worth of fish. If you don't do something about it, I will go to the fish store down the street.

I hope to see you, soon.

Another funny thing about the letter is that I almost sandwiched the bad news. Remember when you write a complaint, start and end with something nice to say. I was a little too harsh in my introduction.

This book is divided into chapters based on experiences I've had as a customer of companies that provided excellent customer service (The Successful), mediocre customer service (The Room for Improvement), and horrible customer service (The Going out of Business). Read this book from cover to cover, taking special note of the situations that apply to your work. For ease of writing, I will play the customer role (written in red) in each situation, and the professional (written in purple) will be a man. Each vignette is based on an actual business transaction. To highlight something really bad or good that was said or done by the professional, you will read, "Strike one" or "Home run," respectively. An explanation will follow. Yes, I love baseball. What I'm *thinking* will be written in italics.

In some situations you may think that I'm being a total bitch or extremely difficult. Good. In the first chapter you'll notice how the elite gracefully handle such a customer compared to the professionals in the other chapters.

CHAPTER 1

THE SUCCESSFUL

Across the board, the characteristics that I found all great professionals to possess are patience and compassion. Whether the customer is talkative, loud, angry, rude, or overly zealous, The Successful handle their patrons with grace, equality, and respect. They listen to what their customers need, which just may be to tell a story about something happening in their life, and then provide the requested service or product as though each customer is the favorite.

Another quality of great professionals is that they leave their baggage at the door. In other words, whatever is bothering them that day, or whatever stress they have in their life, they clear their mind of it before they start work. There are many benefits to this practice. One is that it's easier to cater to others' needs when you are not thinking about your own. Second, you are less likely to talk about yourself with customers and more likely to focus on their needs. Remember, most people either don't care about your bad news or they're glad to hear it.

My favorite effect of leaving my baggage at the door was experienced when I offered one-hour personal training sessions at clients' homes. At the end of each hour, I walked out of my client's home floating. It was great stress management. For that one hour (and I had several appointments each day), I had no care in the world. Imagine having the skill to let go of your worries for eight hours each day!

Enjoy the vignettes. Maybe you can put into practice the techniques of The Successful.

At a dance club, speaking to bar owner.

Hi. I heard a lot of great things about your place and was excited to dance, tonight, but the music is prohibitively loud even with my ear plugs. I don't want to be a cheapskate, but I would like to be refunded the cover charge. I've only been here 15 minutes.

I would be happy to refund your money. I am so sorry that the music is too loud for you. I do hope that you come back. We have different types of music during the week; maybe another day will work better for you.

As I said goodbye, he took my hand into both of his hands and graciously thanked me for coming. Home run.

Home run: The bar owner was genuine and truly valued my business.

At a hair salon speaking to a stylist.

Do you take walk-ins?

Sometimes.

Sometimes? That seems weird to me. It seems like you either do or you don't as a rule, and then if you do, you either have time or you don't.

Maybe I am being a little too literal.

Yes, I take walk-ins, and I have time to work with you right now. Home run.

Home run: Even though I was being too literal, he patiently accepted my rhetoric and enthusiastically accepted me as a new client.

Speaking with a restaurant owner.

I have been to your restaurant many times, but before now, no one has explained why the blue cheese salad dressing contains gluten.

The blue cheese dressing is made with tarragon vinegar.

Tarragon is an herb. I wonder why the vinegar is not gluten free.

I'll be right back.

He returns with the container of tarragon vinegar. Home run.

Let's see. Oh, look at the label. It says malt vinegar, which is from barley. That's why the blue cheese dressing is not gluten free.

I am happy to double check anything for you. I learned something new. Home run.

Home runs: The restaurant owner not only went out of his way to educate me and make me feel safe, but also he humbly embraced learning something new.

Speaking with an airport administrator.

Hi. I can't find the airport shuttle.

It's right over here. Follow me.

He walks me through baggage claim, out the door, to the shuttle stop, and directs a shuttle employee to take care of me. Home run.

Home run: The administrator could have just given me directions, but he went out of his way to escort me to the shuttle stop. Consider every customer request and task a convenience to you, and you will convey that you are serving the customer.

Speaking on the phone with an auto body repair shop manager.

Hi. This is Jeanne Murdock. I've been to your shop before. I'm not sure if you remember me.

Sure, I remember you. 1997 Toyota T100. Home run #1.

Yes! Now I have some nicks in my truck that I'd like you to fix.

OK Bring it down and we'll look at it right away. Home run #2.

I take the truck in, leave it overnight, and return the next day.

Wow! It looks great!

Yes, we just buffed out the nicks and washed the car for you. Home run #3.

Very good. Thank you. How much do I owe you?

Nothing. You're a valued customer. Home run #4.

Just tell your friends about us. Home run #5.

Home run #1: By remembering my truck and me, the manager made me feel like I was a valued customer.

Home run #2: He made me feel like a high priority by wanting to help me right away.

Home run #3: Washing the car was making an extra effort. This is an example when someone deserves a tip, as opposed to someone just doing his job, like a cab driver taking me from point A to point B.

Home run #4: Stating that I'm a valued customer enforced my feeling of such. You can't just state the fact, though; valuing a customer is an action.

Home run #5: The manager was smart enough to ask for future business. Word of mouth is the best way to get more customers.

Speaking with a restaurant employee.
I open the door to the restaurant. I haven't walked in, yet.
Hi. How can we help you? Home run.

Home run: I hadn't even walked into the restaurant, yet,
and I was already being greeted. I felt like they were so
excited to see me. I felt like they were looking forward to
seeing me, even though we had never before met.

Speaking with a store cashier.
He is scanning my items.
Could you please turn down the beeper?
Oh, sure, honey. Home run #1.
Thank you. The other cashiers always tell me, "No."
What?! You just tell them that I said to turn it down for
you. Home run #2.

Home run #1: The cashier graciously tended to my request.
Home run #2: The cashier put forth effort to make sure that
my future store visits would be pleasurable. He also took
the initiative to make sure that the other cashiers treated me
well, even though he didn't actually have authority over
them.

Speaking with a waiter.
I walk in.
Hi, Jeanne. Home run #1.
Hi.
Chicken and broccoli? Home run #2.
Yes, please.

Home run #1: The waiter greeted me right away and remembered my name.
Home run #2: The waiter remembered my order. Not only is restaurant food that tastes homemade wonderful, but so is being treated like I'm welcomed in their "home."

Speaking with a store cashier.
Your total is $15.34.
Here's $20.
Would you like to donate the sixty-four cents to our fundraiser?
He explains the fundraiser.
No, but I would if it were for celiac disease.
Oh, that would be great. I wish that we were raising money for celiac disease. More and more people are finding out that they have it. Home run.

Home run: The cashier acknowledged what I said and was familiar with the condition. He should be. Celiac disease is why the store is stocked with so many gluten-free products. The cashier also seemed enthusiastic about raising money for celiac disease, which made me feel like he cared about what was important to me.

Speaking with an auto shop owner.
I know that you normally do body work here, but would you be willing to change my spark plugs?
Sure, we can do that for you. Home run #1.
Is it OK if I watch? I really want to learn how to do it myself.
Sure, one of my mechanics will explain each step as he changes the plugs. Home run #2.
Perfect. Thank you so much.

Home run #1: The shop owner made an exception for me, which felt like I was receiving special treatment.
Home run #2: The shop owner was wise enough to focus on the sale that he could make now, rather than the future sales that he would not be making from me, since I would be doing the work myself. He knew that not only would I make his shop my first choice in the future when I couldn't do something myself, but also that I would continue referring other people to him.

TAPS Truck & Auto Accessories, Inc.
1207 13th Street
Paso Robles, CA 93446
805-226-8277
www.tapstruckaccessories.com

Speaking with an employee of a clothing store.
Hi, I bought a top similar to this one last month and I'm really unhappy with it.
What's wrong with it?
I explain in a whiny, frustrated voice for a couple of minutes.
He listens. Home run #1.
Maybe you would like this top better. Home run #2.
I'll think about it. What is your return policy?
Within 30 days you can exchange any item if it still has the tags attached, and you have your receipt. Home run #3.
OK, well, I've already worn the item.
Would you like to try on this top?
No, but I'll think about it. Thank you.

Home run #1: The employee let me vent without interrupting and without being defensive.
Home run #2: Then, he offered another option, which is a great way to distract people from their frustration.
Home run #3: He explained the return policy and then went right back to offering another item, rather than defending the store's rules.

Speaking with a grocery store's food service worker.

Hi, Can I help you?

Yes. I'd like the teriyaki beef bowl, please.

While I'm waiting for my food to cook, another worker walks up to me.

Hi, Can I help you?

I've been helped, thanks.

Two other people walk up to me and ask the same question. A total of four people checked on me in a span of ten minutes. Home run.

Home run: I felt like I was the most important person in the store, and as though four people were waiting on me. Always make sure that a customer has been helped and acknowledged immediately, no matter how busy you are.

Speaking with the owner of a gas station.
Hi, how have you been?
I've been doing great, thank you.
I haven't seen you in a while. Home run #1.
I've been traveling a lot.
Are you filling up with regular unleaded?
Yes.
I'll get that for you. Home run #2.
Would you like me to check your oil?
No, thanks. I just checked it.
Can I wash your windows for you?
No, thanks. I'm waiting for it to rain.

Home run #1: The owner is a very hands-on businessman.
He isn't one of those people who only cares about his bank
account. The owner made a point to come right out of the
office to greet me when I pulled up. When he said that he
hadn't seen me in a while, he made me feel missed and
important.
Home run #2: The owner filled up my tank, even though I
was in the self-serve lane. Be bold enough to get your
hands dirty, figuratively and literally, in order to make
someone feel like a valued customer. Coddling your
customer goes a long way.
Spring St. Mobil
1339 Spring St.
Paso Robles, CA 93446
805-238-6315
www.springstreetmobil.com

Speaking with a shop owner.
Jeanne! Where've you been? I missed you. Home run #1.
I've been traveling a lot.
You look great.
Thank you.
Let me show you what new items came in since you were
last here. Home run #2.

Home run #1: The owner made me feel missed and like a
valued customer.
Home run #2: Not only was he wise enough to update me
on his merchandise, but also *he* was the one to escort me
through the store, rather than sending me off on my own.

Speaking with a consultant.
Do you know which exercise equipment manufacturers are
based in California?
I don't know, but I can research it for you. I have to charge
extra for research. Do you still want me to do it for you?
Home run.
No, thanks. I'll look it up myself.

Home run: Anytime a customer asks you a question that
you don't know, offer something more than just, "No."
Offer to research the question and get back to the customer
in a specified time frame. Be honest and disclose in
advance of the research whether or not you have to charge
for your time. When you inform a customer that there will
be an extra charge, you give her the opportunity to say
either, "That's fine" or "No, thanks." Never assume that a
customer knows all of your service charges and don't
surprise a customer with a bill.

Speaking with a storage facility employee.
Do you have any units available?
Yes, which size would you like?
Before I choose a size I would like to know what your
policies are.
Twenty questions later, he is still patiently and graciously
answering my questions. Home run.

Home run: The employee was so patient with me, as
though I was the most important customer of the day.
When a worker or business owner is impatient with my
questions, I wonder two things: What are you hiding? and
Do you have something better to do?

Speaking with a moving company owner.
I just found out that I have to move in a few days. Do you have time to help me?
Since you are a returning customer, I'll make time for you. Home run #1.
Are you charging the same amount as before?
I am charging more, but since you're a valued customer, I want to give you a good deal. Home run #2.

Home run #1: The owner made me feel like I was his number one priority and that I could count on him anytime. How many people do you know in your professional or personal lives who will help you at a moment's notice when you're in a bind? Knowing that you can count on certain people definitely creates peace of mind.
Home run #2: The owner found a second opportunity to tell me that I was a valued customer. He was also respectful and conscious of the total amount that he would charge me. I like it when business owners set aside their excitement for how much they're earning and sympathize with my having to spend money on something that is an unpleasant experience.

Speaking with an airport parking lot shuttle driver.

Hi. I am on my way to your parking lot right now. How can I take advantage of your online coupon if I don't have a printer?

I'm just a driver who is helping out with the phone for a couple minutes. Speak with the parking attendant when you arrive. She's really nice. Home run #1.

When I drove up, the parking attendant was prepared with a printed coupon for me. Home run #2.

Home run #1: Complimenting your co-workers *and* saying nice things about them to your customers goes a long way. Customers want to patronize businesses where the atmosphere is light and positive, not where there's tension and animosity.

Home run #2: The driver took the time to tell the parking attendant to expect me, which gave the attendant the opportunity to give me not only a special welcome, but also a special deal. I felt like they had rolled out the red carpet for me. When I told the parking attendant that her co-worker said nice things about her, she smiled from ear to ear. It doesn't take much to make someone feel good, create comradery, and improve job satisfaction.

Speaking with a bartender.
I considered what you have to drink, but there is nothing that suits me. Can I please use my laptop here and just give you a donation?
You don't have to give me a donation. Just have at it.
Home run.

Home run: The bartender was smart enough to allow me to use his business location to work, knowing that I might change my mind and order a drink. Or, maybe I would come back another day and, who knows, bring a bunch of my friends. When you focus on the business that you could receive, rather than dwell on the business you're not receiving at that moment, you become much more successful. Even if I never return, I will spread the word about the bar as a nice place to socialize. Remember that word of mouth is the least expensive, most effective form of advertising. Make sure that people leave your business with something nice to say about it.

Speaking with a dental hygientist's secretary.
We have an opening today. Would you like to come in?
Oh, shoot. I can't. I'm out of town.
I know that today isn't one of the days that you said that you could come in, but I thought I'd give you a call, anyway. Home run.

Home run: It's nice to know that someone is keeping me in mind and looking forward to serving me. Keep in touch with your customers who are on a waiting list, even if it's not their turn, yet. Let them know that you're thinking about them and that you appreciate their patience. The phone call will also keep you in the forefront of your customers' mind, which may make them less likely to stray to a different business.

Speaking with a motel owner.

Hi. I have a reservation for today. Murdock.

Oh, you're early. Really early.

Yes, I flew the red eye last night.

Oh, you must be tired.

Very.

Well, check in is not until 3 p.m.

Yes.

Check out is 11 a.m., so I'll have your room cleaned first and get you in at 11:30 a.m. Home run.

That would be great. I'll be back at 11:30 a.m.

Home run: The owner was sensitive enough to notice that I looked like I hadn't slept in a week and gracious enough to get me a room as soon as possible. Don't be afraid to make exceptions for customers. It's not like you have to post a sign that says, "Any policy may be broken by anyone at anytime."

Speaking with a waiter.
Can I please have an omelet?
We only serve omelets during breakfast. But, I can see if the chef feels like making one. Home run #1.
You can see if the chef feels like earning money.
He goes back to the kitchen and returns.
The chef is on his break. I'll just make it for you. I used to be a chef. Home run #2.

Home run #1: The waiter was wise enough to see passed his rote answers, knowing that if I didn't get to eat an omelet, then I wouldn't order anything at his restaurant.
Home run #2: The chef went way beyond his duties to make my lunch. He was even knowledgeable about the gluten-free diet, because his mom eats as such. Telling me about his mom's similar dietary restrictions was like saying, "You're not alone. I understand."

Speaking with a waiter.
Can I please have milk?
Sure. I'll be right back.
He brings the milk and checks on me a few minutes later.
That was perfect. Thank you.
Don't worry about the check. It's on us. Home run.

Home run: How generous to give me my drink for free. Also, I appreciated that he didn't give me any snide look or resentment for not ordering alcohol in a bar. He forwent his immediate tip and bar's profit, knowing that there may be a financial gain in the future from me and others I will tell about the exceptional service.

Speaking with a grocery store employee.
We're in the parking lot and he's rounding up the shopping carts that people were too lazy to return to the corrals.
Don't you get tired of people leaving carts everywhere, like that lady? She just put the cart in a planter box.
It's my job. I don't mind. Home run #1.
People are so lazy.
Maybe she wasn't feeling well, today, and didn't want to have to walk far. Home run #2.

Home run#1: The employee had the opportunity to bad mouth a customer, but he didn't.
Home run#2: I even gave the employee a second chance to say something negative but, instead, he gave the customer the benefit of the doubt. Never say anything negative to customers about other customers, because you instill the thought that you will say something negative about them to the next customer. Besides, it's disrespectful.

Speaking with a waiter.
Here's your check.
Thank you. What is the percent sales tax here?
It's seven percent. Home run.

Home run: I would say that 100% of the time, besides this occasion, that I ask store employees, especially waiters, what their percent sales tax is they don't know. How is that possible? Actually, I have found that most people of a community don't even know what their city's percent sales tax is. Workers should definitely know. Are their bosses not telling them? Do the bosses even know? The percent sales tax should be printed on the receipt, because your customer should know how much you're charging.

Speaking with a store cashier.
The total is $56.11.
Here is my credit card.
He reads it, swipes it, and gives it back to me.
Thank you, Miss Murdock. Home run.

Home run: Always address customers by their last name.
Maintaining formalness, without giving yourself
permission to use someone's first name, is classy. It is
alright, though, to ask, "Would you like me to call you
Jeanne or Miss Murdock?" Sometimes it's difficult to
remember who wants to be called what, so when in doubt,
use a customer's last name. For women, choosing a title
when you don't know the person's preference is a
challenge, since there are three choices: Ms., Mrs., and
Miss. I always use Miss when I don't know. Since people
like to hear their name, use it often. "Hello, Miss
Murdock." "Well, Miss Murdock, I think that this option is
the best for you." "Thank you for your business, Miss
Murdock."

Speaking with a hotel shuttle driver.
I check out of one hotel and need to check into a different one three miles away.
Can you please take me to another hotel?
We normally only drive to and from the airport, but since the other hotel is close, I'll take you—no extra charge.
Home run.

Home run: The driver bent the rules to be accommodating and to make me feel special. He took me off of his route—to a competitor—and didn't charge me anything for the ride. What I valued most is that he did not say anything negative or act resentfully about my checking out of his hotel and into another. This great service and positive attitude ensured my return to his hotel in the future.

Speaking with a gas station worker.
Can I please use your restroom?
Sure, here's the key. The bathroom is right around the corner.
Thank you.
A few minutes later I return with the key.
Thank you.
I leave the gas station without buying anything.
Have a good day. Home run.
You, too.

Home run: I do understand why some businesses want to offer the restroom to customers only, but accommodating others may foster new customers. Also, keep in mind that just because someone didn't buy anything from you that day, that time that she used the restroom, doesn't mean that she isn't a customer. The person may have purchased from you in the past. In the case of this gas station, I didn't buy anything that day, but I did in the past. Also, as a thank you, I purchased gas from them the next day, even though the price was a little higher than the stations down the street.

Speaking with a musician at a restaurant.

I saw what happened to you earlier. You were kicked out weren't you?

Yes. The waitress said that I couldn't eat the food I brought in.

That's what I figured. I was going to tell her, "What if she has a food allergy or can't eat gluten?"

Really? Aw. You're right. I can't eat gluten.

They don't have anything you can eat here, right?

Right.

I was going to tell the waitress, "Let her stay. She bought a drink!" Home run.

You're going to make me cry.

Home run. This was a situation of a business within a business. The musician was hired to play at a restaurant. Not only did he provide an exceptional service of entertainment, but also he was trying to enhance the experience that the restaurant was providing—or should have been providing. He didn't end up speaking to the waitress, but he did do damage control by talking with me, sympathizing, and trying to make me feel better. He wanted to make sure that I left his concert and the restaurant on a positive note and with a smile on my face. Doing damage control in another business is an interesting phenomenon. I've done it before. One time that I did damage control was in a cruise ship's restaurant. Some cruise goers were treating the waiters like crap, even though the waiters were providing five-star service. I made a point to talk with the waiters to ensure them that they were great and not to doubt their customer service skills.

Speaking with a store clerk.
I need to return this blender.
OK. Do you have a receipt?
No.
Then, I'll be happy to give you a store credit. Home run.
Thank you.

Home run: The clerk didn't make me feel guilty for
returning something or for not having the receipt.
Allowing returns doesn't work for some merchandise, like
lingerie, but the policy does allow customers to purchase
with confidence. Make sure that your return policy is
clearly stated and familiarized by each customer. I can
understand why stores don't like returns, but you can
handle the policy with grace—without making a customer
feel guilty, lectured, uncomfortable, or embarrassed. Then,
interest the customer in something else. "I'm sorry that this
item didn't work for you, but allow me to show you what
new inventory came in since you were last here." Think of
a return as a gift--the customer came into your store, again!
You have another opportunity to sell merchandise.

Speaking with an event organizer.

I'm reading on your website that you don't allow outside food or drinks.

Yes, that's right. We're having a fundraiser. Home run #1.

Is it alright if I bring a few snacks? I have to be on a special diet, and I can't eat your food.

Oh, sure. I understand. Just ask for me at the entrance. Home run #2.

Thank you so much.

Home run #1: The event organizer didn't defend or explain his policy. I didn't ask why, anyway. He was just confirming what I said.

Home run #2: He was very accommodating and compassionate. Plus he knew that he could miss out on a lot more than the few dollars if he said that I couldn't bring food; he would have lost my entrance fee and that of four members of my family.

Speaking with a store cashier.

You have some really good sales, today.

Yes, we do. Home run.

Home run: Short but sweet. Also, the cashier didn't say, "We do?" He was well aware of his store's sales.

Speaking with a butcher.
Do you have ground turkey without additives?
Yes, it's right here.
Perfect.
Do you know why this meat looks different from that meat?
No.
Oh, great! This will be a learning experience for you!
Home run.

Home run: The butcher not only gave me all of his attention, but also much of his time, making me feel like I was his favorite customer. More importantly, he was so excited to teach me about the different meats—even after he knew about my nutrition background. I was so impressed by his confidence and his love of teaching. The more your customers know about your products, the more likely your customers will form a connection to them and want to own them. Also, the more they know, the more likely they will make the right purchase—of a product that won't be returned.

Speaking with a pharmacist at a meeting.

You know a lot more about gluten in medications than other pharmacists I've met. Can I contact you the next time I have a question that my pharmacist can't answer? Absolutely. Anytime.

The thing is . . . I have an insurance plan that doesn't allow me to patronize your business. So, unfortunately, I can't buy my pills from you.

No problem at all. We want to help the community any way we can. Home run.

Home run: This vignette is a great example of a business owner going above and beyond his normal job and customer service responsibilities. He views the nearby residents and himself as one unit that is strong if everyone plays a role in helping others. He's also smart enough to know that even if I can't buy from him, I will know a lot of people who can.

Speaking with a store owner.

Hi. Can I please have change for a dollar for the parking meter?

Sure. No problem. Here you go. Home run.

I go outside and put change in the meter and then go back into the store. And, guess what happens.

Home run: I went into the closest store to my car to get change for the parking meter. Even though I didn't care to shop and had little interest in the store, I showed gratitude by going back into the shop to see what the retailer offered. A few minutes later, I walked out with a pair of sandals that I didn't know I needed. The store owner was smart enough to know that assisting people like me can turn a non-customer into a new customer. You should view everyone as a potential customer and advocate for your business.

In the above scenarios, you read a variety of situations, several different mindsets of mine, and how The Successful handled each experience gracefully. I left each business looking forward not only to return, but also to recommend the company to others.

CHAPTER 2

THE ROOM FOR IMPROVEMENT

When I was ten years old, I couldn't wait to start working. I promised myself that I would only work at a job I loved, and that if I ever stopped liking my job, I would quit. I knew that there was a direct correlation between liking my job and treating customers well. I think that some of the professionals in this chapter really do mean well; they just don't like their job.

There are so many good businesses and professionals who could be even more successful if they would just make simple adjustments to how they serve and address the customer. The alterations are so easy and make a huge difference. Be mindful of what you're saying and how you're acting.

At a restaurant, speaking to waiter.

Here is your change.

The total was $21.61 and I gave you $40. You gave me $18 change. Where's the rest of it?

My boss told me never to give coins. Either round up or round down.

I can see rounding up, but not rounding down. You shorted me.

He left the table and quickly returned with the rest of my change.

Tell your boss that one of your customers said that she thinks it's totally unacceptable to short change her.

Well, I think my boss wants us to round, because . . . Strike one.

I don't need an explanation. I just want you to tell him that I think it's unacceptable to short change me.

Strike one: Don't explain the reasons behind your policies. If you explain without being asked, it makes you sound defensive. Also, explanations provide customers the opportunity to argue with you. No matter what you say, some customers will argue every point you make about your policies. When asked for a reason about a particular policy, just say, "That's just what works best for us."

Speaking with the man I hired to build a fence around my yard.

I've never before hired anyone to build a fence, so I'm not sure what my choices are, especially for a two-acre property.

You can have anything you want. Strike one. You can have a fence made out of wood, fiberglass, pipe, and wire, for example. Which kind do you want?

I don't know. Which is the least expensive?

Wire.

What are my choices with wire?

There are two different sizes. You can have anything you want.

Which do you recommend?

The smaller size, but it's up to you. Strike two.

Strike one: Customers like knowing that they can have anything they want, but you don't actually have to state such unless asked.

Strike two: I know that it's up to me. My questions were for the purpose of collecting information. How do I know what I want if I don't have all of the information I need to make a decision? I notice that some professionals will say, "It's up to you" or "You can have anything you want" out of discomfort. But, why are they uncomfortable? I know that some professionals don't like questions, but there must be something else.

Talking with a bank teller.

I just need your home address to confirm that this is your account.

I'll write it down for you, because I don't care to publicize my address.

I hand him the paper.

OK So, your address is 1234 Main St.? Strike one.

Yes. I didn't want my address read out loud.

Oh, sorry. I just wanted to make sure that I could read your writing.

Can you please write down my balance now?

You have $100 left in your account. Strike two.

Thanks for telling everyone where I live and that I'm broke.

I sulk away.

Strike one: Don't vocalize a customer's address when there are other customers nearby. You should always maintain a customer's privacy. If you aren't sure about a particular number or letter written on the paper, show the paper to the customer and ask about the digit in question.

Strike two: Vocalizing the amount of money that a customer has in her account leaves her vulnerable for physical or identity theft.

Talking with a car wash cashier.
That'll be $4.99.
Here you go.
Out of $5?
Yes.
He places my $.01 change in the penny cup. Strike one.

Strike one: Penny cups are convenient for placing unwanted change or taking a coin to round out the bill. In this case, the cahier made the mistake of assuming that I wanted to donate my change to the cup. *Never* assume. *Always* give customers their full change. If a customer wants to donate their change, let them take action, which makes them feel empowered and virtuous.

Listening to a lecturer, who is nearing the end of his presentation.
While I still have your attention, I'd like to plug my book.
Strike one.

Strike one: He shouldn't have said, "plug," because it sounds as though he thinks that he is inconveniencing his audience. Maintain the idea that people benefit from your products and services and that they are anxiously waiting to own what you offer. The lecturer could have *shared* information about his book. Also, *plug* can make people uneasy as though they are about to be sold something.

Speaking with a masseur.
I told you that I charge $65 per hour, but I actually charge $75. I forgot that I increased my rate. I will honor my original quote. Home run.
But, you're getting a really good deal. Strike one.

Home run: He did well keeping his word by charging the original quote.
Strike one: You don't have to highlight that your customer is getting a good deal. She can do the math. Stating such sounds engrained and resentful. "I'm giving you a good deal, but I'm going to hold it against you."

Speaking with a bicycle mechanic.
I can't figure out why my bike is making a crunching noise.
He offers a few possible reasons.
I ask more questions.
One of his co-workers approaches and starts answering my questions, silencing the first mechanic. Strike one.
I continue to address the first mechanic, but the co-worker continues to answer my questions. Strike two.

Strike one: The co-worker offered his advice without my asking his opinion. The co-worker also depleted the first mechanic's credibility by disallowing him to answer my questions. "He doesn't know anything, so I'll help you."
Strike two: Even though I continued to direct my questions to the first mechanic, the co-worker controlled the conversation. If you think that a co-worker needs your assistance with a customer, ask.

Speaking with a store cashier.
Before my transaction begins.
Do you accept out of state checks?
I don't know. We'll see if the machine takes it. Strike one.
The items are rung up and my total is given.
I write the check and hand it to the cashier.
Can I see your ID?
Sure.
I might need your physical address. There is a P.O. box on your check. Let me ask my supervisor.
The supervisor states that he can't accept my check, because my ID doesn't have a physical address.
This is why I asked you *before* I wrote the check. Now I've wasted a check. I'm traveling with only one check left, now.
I didn't know that your check and ID had only a P.O. box.
Strike two.

Strike one: The cashier didn't know the store's check policy. You should know your company's policies backwards and forwards and how you should handle every possible scenario.
Strike two: The cashier put the blame on me. He should have said, "Sorry, I should have been more familiar with our store's check policy."

Speaking with a store clerk.
I walk up to the counter. He's on the phone with a customer. I wait patiently.
He motions with his hand like he's trying to get the customer on the phone to hurry the conversation. Strike one.
He finishes the call and hangs up the phone.
Sorry about that. That customer is such a pain in the ass.
Strike two.

Strike one: Watching the clerk motion his hand made me wonder if he does that while I am on the phone with him. I am going to wonder that every time I call. Patience goes a long way in business and makes customers think that your day revolves around them.
Strike two: Don't *ever* say anything negative or derogatory about a customer to another customer. It makes you look bad and ungrateful of a customer's patronage. These negative comments also make me wonder if they are used on me when I'm not around.

Speaking with a produce vendor.
Is this fruit sweet?
Oh, yes. All of our fruit is sweet. It's the sweetest. Strike one.
I don't like sweet; I like tart.

Strike one: Know what your customers want and need before you sell them a particular product. It's called qualifying. After I asked if the fruit were sweet, he should have asked, "Do you prefer sweet fruit?" It's alright to answer a question with a question, so that you can direct a customer toward the most appropriate product. Instead, he completely lost my attention and interest in his produce.

Speaking with a banker.

I just need you to sign this form. Strike one.

Sure.

I start reading the form.

You just need to sign right here. Strike two.

I start reading from the top, again.

It just states that you . . . Strike three.

I start reading from the top, again.

You just need to sign right there. Strike four.

Do you not want me to read what I'm about to sign?

Of course. Strike five.

I can't concentrate on what I'm reading when you're talking.

Strike one: Don't say "sign," because it sounds like too big of a commitment. "I need you to sign over your whole life to me." Just say, "I need your signature" or "I need you to OK this form."

Strike two: I saw the signature line the first time he pointed to it.

Strike three: It's alright to summarize a form when you are handing it to someone, but after that Shhh! Let the customer read the form.

Strike four: He was being very impatient. Was he uncomfortable with silence or was there something unethical about his form?

Strike five: As a rule, don't answer a question with "of course." It's like saying, "That was a dumb question."

Speaking with a book seller.
This looks like an interesting book. Tell me about it.
He tells me.
I start flipping through the pages.
He keeps talking while I peruse the book. Strike one.

Strike one: Shhh! Once you have answered a customer's questions, Shhh! The customer can't focus on the product if you're talking the whole time. Also, a customer's thinking may involve talking oneself into buying the product. Why would you want to interrupt that thought process? Nothing you say will be more convincing than one's own thinking. Learn to love silence.

Speaking with a store clerk.
We finish the transaction.
Thank you. See you later.
Thanks for coming in. Don't forget that we're getting our
new inventory next week. Strike one.

Strike one: Instead of saying "don't forget," say
"remember." "Remember that we're getting our . . ." The
brain only hears key works like forget and remember.
What I heard was, "Forget that we're getting our . . ." So, I
forgot.

Speaking with a store cashier.
He is scanning my items.
I plug my ears, because the beeper is too loud.
He continues. Strike one.
Can you please turn down the beeper?
No. If I turn it down I can't hear it. Strike two.
I can hear it from the other side of the store.

Strike one: Pay attention to your customers. The cashier
was just acting like a robot scanning my items. Maybe he
was thinking about his upcoming cigarette break. Make
your customers' store experience a pleasurable one, so that
they will want to return.
Strike two: Put your customers' needs before your own. I
used to personal fitness train a man in his house that he
kept at 60^0 F. while he exercised. That temperature felt like
the Arctic Circle to me. Instead of asking him to heat his
house, I brought a thick jacket—even in the middle of
summer.

Speaking with a carpet salesman.
Hi. I'd like to order new carpeting for my house.
OK We have a lot of options for you. He lists I don't know how many. He lost my attention after the first three. Strike one.

Strike one: It's nice to have a lot of options for your customers, but you don't have to list them all. Doing so just confuses customers and loses their attention. Instead, ask questions to determine what their needs and likes are. Once you have the information you need, select several options. Keep the selections in your head and then share just what you think will be the best choice. If the customer doesn't like it, then go onto the second best choice. Continue this process until the customer says, "Yes."

Speaking with a store cashier.
Hi.
Hi.
How are you?
Terrible. My mom just died. [Inside joke between my mom and me, but true.]
Silence. Strike one.
OK That'll be $45.80.

Strike one: I know that busy cashiers don't have time to listen to someone's sob story, but they can at least acknowledge the response and offer some sympathy. Also, I believe that in any personal or professional situation you shouldn't ask, "How are you?" unless you have the interest and time to hear the answer and explanation.

Speaking with a store cashier.
Hi.
Hi.
Did you find everything OK?
No. [Most cashiers stop here.]
What were you looking for?
I tell him.
He gives a blank stare. Strike one.
OK That'll be $25.61. Strike two.

Strike one: You need to know your store inventory
backwards and forwards. A cheat sheet is alright to have,
though. There should be either a book or computer
database where you can search for a product.
Strike two: The cashier offered no solution for supplying
me with the items that I wanted. He could have offered to
order them, or he could have provided alternative items.
My sum total would have been greater if someone would
have been available to walk the aisles with me, looking for
what I wanted. Turn customers on to what you currently
carry and point out new merchandise. Pay attention to their
demands. Your business's survival is based on how much
you sell. When customers tell you what they want, they're
handing you success on a silver platter.

Speaking with a bank teller.
Hi.
Hi. I need to deposit a check.
OK I can help you with that.
I'm surprised that you're allowed to chew gum.
I'm not. Strike one.
He looks over his shoulder. Strike two.

Strike one: Don't keep employees who defy your company's policies. You may be at fault, though. You, too, have to practice your company's policies—always—and be consistent with enforcing them.
Strike two: The teller showed that he had no problem being deceptive, either. This action makes me lose trust in him. I wished I hadn't given him my account number.

Speaking with a fabric store clerk.

I walk into the store. One worker is eating an ice cream sandwich in between talking with customers, while the other worker is playing with his mobile phone. Strike one.

Do you work here?

Ya'. Strike two.

Oh, I wasn't sure. Do you sell foam?

Ya'. What size do you need?

I'm not sure. What are my choices?

He hands me a sign with sizes and prices.

What are the units? There are numbers, but it doesn't state feet or inches.

He grabs the sign out of my hands. Strike three.

Just tell me how thick you want it. Hold up a finger. Strike four.

I'll hold up a finger alright.

I know what two inches looks like.

It would be good to write "inches" on this paper.

Silence. Strike five.

Which one do you want me to get?

The one that's one inch by 24 inches by 48 inches.

He leaves and returns with the foam.

While I'm deciding if I like it or not, a lady walks up and asks the clerk if he works here.

I'm noticing a trend.

I'll have to take measurements at home and then return tomorrow.

OK, but this is the last one left. Strike six.

Strike one: Don't eat in front of customers. It's really tacky, unless you're in an environment where you don't get a break, and you can't leave your post. In this case, be discreet. Also, always look alert and ready to help customers. What you do when there is no one in the store is one thing, but as soon as someone walks in the door, all attention goes to her.

Strike two: Not "ya'." "Yes." Learn to speak well and practice good manners. When you speak articulately, you sound knowledgeable, which can breed trust.

Strike three: *Never* grab anything from a customer. Instead ask, "Can I please see it?"

Strike four: Don't insult your customer's intelligence. Since you don't know what people know, ask. The only assumption you should make is that the customer wants excellent service. Also, be patient. What's the hurry when no one else is in the store?

Strike five: Implement some of the suggestions that customers make. They're telling you how you can make more money from others and themselves. Say, "That's a good suggestion. Thank you for telling me." Plus, you didn't have to pay for the idea.

Strike six: Don't threaten your customers. It's like he said, "You can come back, but it won't do any good. This one won't be here." Why does it matter if that one is still there or not? I don't even know if I need it. Just say, "I'll look forward to seeing you tomorrow."

Speaking with a night club bouncer.

I check the club's website for their music schedule, but it's outdated.

I call and listen to the club's recording for this week's schedule, but it's confusing.

I call and speak with a waitress. She doesn't know if there is a band or a DJ.

I show up at the club, anyway.

I explain my confusion to the bouncer.

I know it's confusing. We sometimes don't know until the last minute if there's a DJ or band. We have live music every Tuesday and Thursday. Wednesdays there's a DJ. It's always been like that for years.

All one big strike.

Strike one: How can your customers patronize your business and receive what they want when they want, if neither you nor they know what you're offering? Keep your website updated. As for the phone recording, state, "This is for the week of . . ." so that people know whether or not the recording is current. The bouncer contradicted himself by saying that they never know when there is a band *and* that their schedule has been the same for years. Customers like consistency and predictability.

Speaking with a food vendor at a convention.
Hi. What are you selling?
He tells me the name of his product.
Oh, I have never heard of that before.
You should know our product, already. Strike one.

Strike one: Don't insult your current and potential customers. You're at the convention to increase awareness, not to demean people for not being familiar with your company. It would be better to say, "Oh, then I would like to familiarize you with our product." Talk about it, let people try it, explain store availability, and then say, "I hope that you will become one of our valued customers."

Speaking with a store stock boy.

I get his attention and wave him over to where I'm standing.

He looks over.

Can I help you? Strike one.

Yes.

He stays put. Can I help you? Strike two.

Yes.

What do you need? Strike three.

Can you come here please?

He rolls his eyes and resentfully walks over. Strike four.

Ya'? Strike five.

I need help from someone who isn't lazy.

Strikes one through three: Don't be so lazy. If anyone looks remotely in need, run don't walk. In fact, don't wait for someone to ask for help. Look around. Say, "Hello" to everyone. Treat customers as though they're in your home. Wait on them. Put your customers' needs before your own and avoid being too focused on finishing your immediate task. I wasn't going to yell my question to the stock boy and, besides, he needs to come to me.

Strike four: *Never* roll your eyes at a customer and remember that what you're thinking is displayed in your body language.

Strike five: "Yes," not "ya'."

Speaking with a grocery store cashier.

Can I please have help in aisle three?

Sure, I'll call someone over.

In a short time, a man walks up with a toothpick in his mouth. Strike one.

Can I help you?

I think I heard him correctly.

Yes, I can't find the dried cherries. Do you have any?

I'll look for you.

There aren't any.

He starts a conversation with me, but I don't follow anything he's saying. The toothpick jumbles his words and performs magic tricks that distract me.

Strike one: The worker was really nice, but the toothpick in the mouth was really tacky. Don't conduct business with a toothpick, gum, hard candy, or anything else in your mouth. Don't chew on a pencil or pen, either. The worker could have hid the toothpick behind his back or tucked it into a pocket. Actually, handling a toothpick that was in your mouth and then touching food is unsanitary. Save the toothpick for your break and then wash your hands.

Speaking with a store employee.

I use the restroom and then walk to the front of the store.

I notice that a lot of your female customers don't wash their hands after using the toilet.

I know. People are disgusting. Strike one.

You should have an alarm that sounds every time someone leaves the restroom without washing one's hands.

I wish we did.

I would invest in that type of alarm before I would invest in a shoplifting alarm.

Strike one: No matter how offensive you find certain customers, don't say negative things about them to co-workers or to another customer. Besides, *every* customer contributes to your paycheck. It would have been alright if the employee said, "That's disgusting." Then, he isn't directing his disdain toward any one person, only an action. His comment made me wonder what he says about me when I'm not present. Maybe, "Jeanne is so hyper; she needs to turn it down a few notches."

Speaking with a store cashier.
This is 50% off, right?
Do you have a club card?
No.
It's only 50% off if you have a club card. Strike one.
Oh, that is so annoying. False advertising makes me so mad.
I would change it if I could.
You can.
No. Corporate makes those decisions.
Yes, but you have a voice. And if they don't listen to you, then there's something seriously wrong with this company.
They didn't tell me that I was transferred here until after I arrived. If I didn't have 13 years with the company, I would have quit. Strike two.

Strike one: I don't expect to be able to change the world of club cards and price tags, but I think that it's terrible to single out customers who don't "belong." While you're making some customers feel special, you're deceiving others and making them feel ripped off and outcast. The club pricing system is entirely confusing, also. It's nearly impossible to look at a product and know what the actual price is, only to be surprised upon check out.
Strike two: I don't care how many years you have with a company, staying at a job you hate affects your health and your ability to care about customers. In the meantime, keep it to yourself. As long as you're an employee, you have an obligation to say only positive things about your company.

Speaking with the receptionist at a repair company.
How much do you charge for a consultation?
We charge $100 per hour with a one-hour minimum.
OK. I'd like to make an appointment.
The repairman comes to my house for one hour, and then says that the bill will be mailed to me.
I receive the bill. I am charged $105. Strike one.
I call the company.
Hi. I'm looking at the bill you sent me, and it states that I owe $105.
Yes, we have a five-dollar fuel charge.
I see that on here. You didn't tell me that when I asked you how much you charge.
Well, we have to charge for fuel; gas is expensive. Strike two.
You can charge whatever you want, but you need to tell me up front.
A fuel charge is an industry standard. Strike three.
I don't need a reason; you just need to tell me up front.

Strike one: *Never* surprise a customer with a bill or for an amount that you didn't disclose in advance of the service. No matter how obvious a charge seems, tell your customer in advance, so that she has the opportunity to say, "No thank you," *before* the service is completed.

Strike two: I didn't ask why the company was charging for fuel. If the receptionist were really listening, he would have heard that I was arguing the fact that I wasn't told up front.

Strike three: "Everybody's doing it" is a lame reason for a business policy. Even if that comment were true, not everyone is withholding fee information at the time of being hired.

Speaking (?) with a store employee.
I am paying for my food at a self-serve kiosk.
A lady yells from a few feet away that I cut in front of her.
I didn't realize that I cut in front of her.
I look over to the kiosk management employee. He recognizes the situation, but says nothing. Strike one.

Strike one: There are some times in life when you should mind your own business. This time was not one of them. The store employee should have intervened to diffuse the situation. Saying something to me could have made me feel better, since I was just yelled at, and saying something to the other customer would have made her feel better, since she felt wronged. The employee could have made a joke to lighten the air or offered special attention. Diffusing the situation is important, because you don't want your customers to associate your store with a bad experience, even if it's just between customers.

Speaking with a sales representative.
Will you please call me when my order is ready?
Of course.
Will you include a receipt with my order?
Of course. Strike one.

Strike one: Saying "of course" is the same as saying, "That's a dumb question." If you want to say an emphatic "yes," then say something like, "Absolutely."

Speaking with store owner.

Hi. I'm calling to find out if my order came in. I left you a message last week.

Oh, yes. I got your message, but I was out sick last week. Strike one.

Well, I left you a message the week before, too.

Oh, I know. I'm much better by email. Strike two.

That doesn't say much, since you never write back.

I sent you several emails, too.

I haven't had the chance to write back, because I've been swamped. Strike three.

He needs my Excuses *book.*

Your order is in. I've been meaning to call you. Strike four.

Strike one: Everyone gets sick once and a while, but you don't need to impose your health problems on your customers. Most people either don't care about your bad news, or they're glad to hear it. It's a cynical perspective, but it's true. Instead, the store owner should have said, "I'm sorry. I should have returned your call right away."
Strike two: As a business owner, you have to be good by email *and* phone. Your communication choices should be based on what your customers prefer, not what you prefer.
Strike three: The store owner is probably not swamped with business, but rather busy work. Many people who are swamped are overcommitted and disorganized—a bad combination for running a business.
Strike four: How can you earn money if you don't provide customers with their merchandise? Customers want their service or product NOW. Get them what the need as quickly as possible, knowing that they may change their mind the longer you make them wait.

Speaking with a store manager.
I would like to return this shirt.
Do you have your receipt?
Yes, here it is.
I see. You bought the shirt three weeks ago.
Yes.
Our return policy is two weeks.
Well, what's one week? Can't you make an exception this one time?
If I do it for you, I have to do it for everyone. Strike one.
No, you don't.

Strike one: How many pet peeves do I have? Oh, well. Add this one to the list, anyway. Losing a customer permanently will cost you much more than making an exception. People want to feel special and believe that you will make an exception for them. No, you don't have to make a particular exception for everyone. It's not like you have to put out a sign that says, "Open for business. All of our policies are negotiable." Or, "Served 1000 exceptions and counting." You don't have to name your business Exceptions Plus—Where Customers Rule. There isn't going to be a mutiny if you make an exception. Have I made my point, yet? I hope not. I'm on a roll.

Speaking with an electrician.

Thanks for the great work today. Do you have a card?

No, I don't have any with me. Strike one.

Here's your money. Can I have a receipt please?

No, I don't have my book with me. I'll mail it to you.
Strike two.

Several phone calls and several lies later, I never received a receipt.

Strike one: *Always* carry business cards with you, especially to a client appointment, which offers a great opportunity for you to generate more leads. Ask your client if she is happy with the work you did and if she would not only hire you again in the future, but also refer you to friends. Ask how many cards she would like and give that exact amount.

Strike two: Always bring a receipt book with you to appointments, unless your business bills people after the work is completed. By now, you may have figured out what the electrician was up to. He was working under the table—avoiding paying income tax. Be an honorable businessman and you will not only reap the rewards, but also avoid bad karma.

Speaking with a masseuse.

Jeanne, we have an appointment for Friday at 3 p.m.

Yes, that's right.

Can we change the appointment to next week? I'm going away for the weekend, and I'd like to leave early to avoid the traffic. Strike one.

Strike one: You shouldn't change client appointments for your own personal or professional convenience. I believe that as far as you're concerned, the appointment is set in stone. You shouldn't change it so that you can have less of a gap between appointments; you can take advantage of a fun opportunity that arose; or you can fit more clients into one day, for example. Besides the fact that changing an appointment means that you're not adhering to your commitment, you inconvenience the client, and give her the opportunity to cancel! You want your client to commit to the appointment, right? Some clients will think about cancelling, but not make the call. Then, if you call to change the appointment, you open the door to a cancellation and, possibly, a decline to reschedule. Certainly, if it is the client's choice to reschedule, you should be gracious, polite, and flexible.

Speaking with a copy center employee.
What are my paper options for copying this flyer?
He tells me.
How much does each cost?
He tells me.
So, what you're saying is, this one costs the most and there are five color choices.
That's what I just said. You want me to explain it all over again?! Strike one.
Geez. Bark at the moon.

Strike one: In this scenario I was practicing effective communication. When you re-word what someone says, you demonstrate your level of understanding. The employee could have responded, "Yes, that's correct" or "Almost." When someone doesn't quite understand me fully, I say, "Almost." Then, I re-explain the part that was not understood. When someone doesn't understand me fully, rather than think the person is of low intelligence, I blame myself for not explaining well.

Speaking with a waiter.

Here is your check.

Thank you.

I read it. There is an extra $2 charge. Strike one.

Wait. What is this $2 charge?

We had to charge you extra, because you wanted chicken instead of shrimp.

After unnecessary further explanation . . .

You should have told me that when I placed my order. The extra charge is not written on the menu.

I'll talk to my manager.

He returns with a new bill—without the extra $2.

Strike one: Never surprise a customer with a bill. You don't have to explain why there has to be an extra charge; you just need to state—in advance—that there will be an extra charge. In the above scenario, the waiter didn't give me the opportunity to say "forget it" or "that's fine." The manager made the right decision when he removed the extra charge from my bill. If he hadn't, I would have taken $2 out of the waiter's tip, and then the waiter would have had to have paid the price of the manager's bad decision. This, in turn, would decrease the waiter's job satisfaction. Another consequence of not removing the extra charge of the bill would have been placing this vignette in chapter 3 of this book.

Speaking with a store cashier.
The total will be $3.50.
I can give you either $3.44 or a twenty. Which would you prefer?
I can't allow everyone to give me less than the total amount. Strike one.
That's not what I asked.
Here's the twenty.

Strike one: The cashier should have just answered, "I'll take the twenty, please." I didn't need an explanation. Also, as I've stated in another vignette, no, you don't have to bend the same rule for everyone. It is alright, though, to make someone feel special. In this scenario, I wasn't at all asking for special treatment; I was just trying to make the cashier's job easier—whichever way that meant.

In the above scenarios you read that most of the professionals were not being mean to me, but I was still dissatisfied with how I was treated. If you've heard yourself speak as some of the above professionals did, ask yourself why. Maybe you have an employer who tells you to speak as such. If so, tell your employer that it not only makes you uncomfortable but, more importantly, the customer. Give examples of dialogue and what the outcome was.

CHAPTER 3

THE GOING OUT OF BUSINESS

I consider schools another example of a business setting. Students are the customers and teachers are the professionals. I could write a whole book on how students should be treated, but I will limit my writing to one example. By the way, why don't college student handbooks include teachers' code of ethics?

If you think that you provide great customer service and that you treat customers well, but your customers complain about how they're treated, then you need to think, again.

When I was 7 years old, I picked flowers from my yard and sold them door-to-door. When I ran out, I streamlined my operational procedures by picking flowers from neighbors' yards and selling them their own flowers. One neighbor asked, "Jeanne, did you pick these from my yard?" I said, "No." Knowing that I was lying, she bought the flowers anyway. I felt so guilty about lying *and* accepting payment that I immediately fired myself from the flower business. And, I haven't lied to a customer since.

Below you'll read a vignette or two where the professional lied to me and what the consequence was. If you ever lie to a customer, assume that you will be fired or, if you're self employed, find the courage to be honest.

Speaking to a furniture store owner.
Oh, what a beautiful mirror! Look at the copper border.
Was that made by a local artist? Look at the detail. It's
absolutely gorgeous. I would love to own it.
It's $1000. It's too expensive. Strike one.

Strike one: He had the sale . . . easily. I sold myself
without him saying a word. All he had to do was ask me
how I wanted to pay for it. Instead, he insulted me by
implying that I couldn't afford it. I was going to buy the
mirror, but I didn't want to help a pompous business owner.
I walked out with nothing, except for the assurance that he
would be out of business within the year. He was.

Speaking with a retirement home receptionist.

I'm walking through the lobby.

Hi.

Jeanne, wait. You need to sign in.

Really? I've been coming here for two years. Now you want me to sign in?

Yes. The resident director said that you need to sign in every time now.

A few weeks later.

I'm sitting in the hallway, resting between appointments.

Jeanne, you can't sit here.

Why not?

The director said that you can't sit here anymore. You have to sit in the lobby.

A few weeks later.

I'm sitting in the lobby.

Jeanne, you can't sit here.

Why not?

The director said that you can't sit here anymore.

Asshole.

Where am I supposed to sit?

I don't know. You just can't sit here anymore. Strike one.

Strike one: Treat customers equally. The resident director obviously held a personal vendetta against me, because he was insecure about how well liked I was by the residents and how professionally successful I was there. If he spent more time caring about the residents, and less time controlling me, he would have had much happier residents. Do you believe in karma? I do. The resident director contracted cancer—twice. His other poor decisions included having an affair with the head of housekeeping, which was unintentionally announced when they dressed as one another for Halloween. What?! Do I have to write a whole chapter on office hanky-panky? The boss-secretary affair is so cliché. What I will say with MUCH passion is this: DO NOT WORK WITH SENIORS FOR THE PAYCHECK. THEY DESERVE PEOPLE WHO ARE PASSIONATE ABOUT HELPING THEM. (And, yes, I am yelling.)

Speaking to a teacher.

Here is your grade for the report. He hands me a torn piece of paper the size of a silver dollar. "Jeanne Murdock 0/50." Strike one.

What is this?

You received zero points, because you didn't hand in a report.

How can this be? I have never in my whole academic career turned in anything late, let alone not at all.

I turned it in. I even turned it in early.

Well, I don't have it.

You must have lost it. I turned it in.

I don't lose papers. Strike two.

You did this time. I'll email it to you when I get home tonight.

OK, but it doesn't mean that I will accept it. It's past due.

I send it to him that night.

Two weeks later mid-sentence during a lecture, laughing:

Oh, Jeanne, I found something of yours. Strike three.

At the end of the lecture, he admits that he found my report in a stack of other papers. I look at my grade. There is a deduction for turning in my report late. Strike four.

Strike one: If you find that you don't have a student's report, especially a good student, talk with the student before giving her a zero. Give students the benefit of the doubt.

Strike two: Don't be so defensive. Admit that you may have made a mistake without blaming the student. Shhh! Listen! Listen to what the student is saying about the scenario.

Strike three: Don't ridicule a student, especially in front of the whole class. Maturely take responsibility for your mistakes.

Strike four: Don't deduct points for a paper that was graded late because you lost it.

Speaking with a computer printer company customer service representative.

Hi. I need help with my printer.

What is it doing?

I explain.

I have no idea what's wrong with your printer. Strike one.

Can I talk with someone who knows about printers?

I know about printers. Strike two.

You just said that you have no idea.

Well, I can help you, but you need to pay for tech support.

Why would I pay you if you have no idea what's wrong with my printer?

The circular arguing continues a couple more rounds.

Strike one: Customer service representatives should know their products backwards and forwards. Relying on computer algorithms doesn't instill customer confidence. Strike two: Don't lie to your customers. When customers know that you're being dishonest, you lose credibility, their trust, and certainly their business.

Speaking with a restaurant owner.
I walk up to the front door.
We're closed. Strike one.
Well, hello to you, too.
We closed at 9. You'll have to come back another time.
Strike two.

Strike one: The first thing you say to a customer should be a greeting. "Welcome. How can I help you?" The owner made me feel like I did something wrong by walking up after he closed. I felt attacked.

Strike two: The owner told me the closing time as though I should have known it, already, and then dictated that I need to return. Here is what would be much better received dialogue: "Hi. How can I help you? Oh, I'm sorry we just closed. Have you been here before? I would love to show you the menu. These are our hours. Would it be more convenient for you to return tomorrow afternoon or evening?" If you had just closed when someone walks up, offer something simple for takeout—something that you can still whip up in your kitchen. The goal is to go out of your way, so that the customer returns.

Speaking with a store cashier.
Hi.
Will that be all?
Yes.
Oh, you found some really cool items.
Oh, I know. I really like your store. I like that—
The cashier's supervisor walks up and starts talking with the cashier. Strike one.
The supervisor berates the cashier for not filling out his time card properly. Strike two.
The supervisor finishes and walks away.
The cashier is dejected.

Strike one: Don't interrupt a conversation—ever. Besides, I was about to issue compliments about the store.
Strike two: *Never* discipline an employee in front of customers *or* other employees. It is disrespectful and rude. It makes you and the employee look bad, and the disciplinary action diminishes the store's credibility and that of the people running it. Leaving your employees with lower self esteem and motivation than before you started talking with them is a good way to lose workers. No workers. No customers. No business.

Speaking with a food manufacturer.

I am looking at your website for product information, but I can't find it.

Did you click on Products?

Yes, but the page didn't state much. I can't find the ingredients or nutrition facts.

Oh, it's not there. The customer isn't going to understand anyway. Strikes one and two.

Strike one: Whether you are selling a product or service, you have an obligation to educate your customers. Learn to be a good teacher. The more information customers have about your business and the industry in general, the more likely they will patronize your company. You *have* to take the time.

Strike two: Insulting your customers' intelligence is a great way to become a statistic—the one about most companies failing within the first year of business.

Speaking with a store owner on the phone.
Hi. This is Jeanne Murdock. I was in your store looking at furniture last week.
Oh, I don't remember. I talk to so many people. Strike one.
I was talking with you about the leather couch. I have another question about it.
Oh, I've shown that couch to so many people. I don't remember. Strike two.

Strikes one and two: The store owner made me feel like a number—a statistic—by telling me that he doesn't remember me *and* by stating that he talks to so many people. If a person doesn't ask if you remember her, and you don't, then you don't have to say that you don't remember. If a person does ask if you remember, say, "I'm sorry I don't remember. Maybe you can jog my memory."

Speaking (or not) with a store clerk.
I walk in. I walk around. Silence. Strike one.
The store clerk is behind the counter.
I walk by the counter. Silence. Strike two.

Strike one: I was not greeted when I walked into the store. You don't need to ambush your customers, but you do need to greet them.
Strike two: My presence was not acknowledged. The clerk and his co-worker were just looking down at some papers. They didn't care that I was in there. It was no wonder that the rest of the store was empty. You can say something like, "Let me know what questions you have." It's also good to point out an item, maybe one that's on sale or new. "I'd like to show you . . ."

Speaking with a home organizer.

Hi. How's business?

It's OK. Strike one.

Have you been busy?

No, not really.

Do you have people calling you for help?

Yes, but they don't call back. Strike two.

Do you follow up with them?

No, if they need me they'll call me. Strike three.

Strike one: Always offer the perception that business is great. Even if it's just an illusion, the more you say it the more you will believe it. The more you believe it the more likely it will be true. Yet, you don't want people to think that you don't have time for them. Say, "Business is booming, and I still have time for new clients."

Strike two: Treat a phone call as a gift. Someone called *you*. The customer is reaching out to you for help. It is your responsibility to listen and to determine how exactly you will help the person. By the end of the phone call, you should have made the first appointment.

Strike three: Some potential customers require years of chasing to get them to work with you. Rarely do potential customers call a second time. You *have to* pursue them. Every time you end a call without an appointment, ask, "When would you like me to follow up with you, again?" Most people will give you a time frame. If they don't, then make up your own schedule and keep calling until the person says, "Please don't call me anymore." If you feel like you're being a pest, then you're doing your job right. If people say, "Thank you for your patience" or "I appreciate your persistence," then you're doing your job right.

Speaking with a business owner.
Hi. I'm Jeanne Murdock. We've met before; I saw you at the last event. *We've actually met more than once before.*
Was I nice? Strike one.
Yes. *Surprisingly.*
That's a first. I'm not normally nice. Strike two.
I know. You're normally indifferent toward me.
I must have been having a rare moment.
That's for sure.

Strike one: "Was I nice?" makes a terrible first (and second, and third, and . . .) impression. He talked through the whole conversation jokingly, but he was actually truthful. He normally is a jerk. Besides, most of what people say when they say that they're just kidding is true. Strike two: Why would anyone want to do business with someone who isn't nice, especially someone who admits it in a first conversation—a first line? I've noticed that the personality and mood of the business owner reflects onto his employees—the whole company. I can tell as soon as I walk into a business, especially a store, if the owner (or on-duty supervisor) is not a nice person. I feel the tension in the air, and then I feel the urge to leave.

Speaking with a store clerk.

I walk into an optical store, which is void of customers.
The man behind the counter is asleep. Strike one.
My perusing awakens the clerk.

Hi.

Hi.

He quickly looks in a mirror and checks his baggy eyes.
Strike two.

No other words are exchanged, and I walk out.

Strike one: Being asleep at the job is never a good thing, especially if you're an air traffic controller or pilot. Good thing the story didn't start with, "I walk into a cockpit . . ." Which comes first? The store has no customers because the clerk is asleep, or the clerk is asleep because there are no customers. When there are no customers in the store, the clerk should conduct tasks, such as cleaning, neatening stock, and bringing in new customers. I notice that a lot of business owners who are struggling to generate revenue, either work a side job or go out of business. These actions have never made sense to me. Why not find more ways to get customers? You obviously have the time to do so if you have time to work a second job. Unless you have the capital to hire a marketing/advertising firm, you need to learn how to be a creative marketer.

Strike two: The clerk could have salvaged his poor welcome by jumping up to help me, rather than tending to his complexion.

Speaking with a museum security guard.
Hi. You have a very nice museum.
Hi. Thank you.
How long have you been working here?
He rolls his eyes and gives a big sigh.
About seven years.
Does that sound like a long time?
Yes.
Why?
I didn't think that I would be working here that long.
Strike one.
What did you think that you would be doing?
I wanted to be a police officer.
Well, can't you still?
No, I'm too old.
Can't you still work for the police department?
I can, but I rather work for harbor patrol.

Strike one: It's one thing to use a job as a stepping stone, but it's another thing to stay at a job you really don't like. I hear a lot of people use the "I need the money" excuse. Suppressing what you really want to do leads to misery, which affects your co-workers and customers. Employers should not only make sure that their employees are happy, but also that their professional growth is as important as the company's growth.   A company full of miserable employees can't survive.

Speaking with a used car salesman.
Hi, I'm calling about the '99 silver van you have for sale.
Oh, sure.
Is it still available?
Yes.
How much is it?
Can you hold please? I'll go check.
Sure.
Five minutes pass. Strike one.
I hang up.

Strike one: It's good to have just enough information, which should include the price, in an ad to entice people to call. But, how can you turn a call into a sale if you can't answer the customer's questions—especially in a timely manner? Five minutes is far too long to keep a customer on hold—especially to find the price. You should have the price at your fingertips. If you know in advance that you need five minutes to find information for a customer, then ask her if she wants to hold for five minutes, or if she wants to hang up and be called back. Give the customer a time frame for when you will call and then adhere to the time exactly. In this scenario, the salesman lost my business, because he kept me on hold too long. I just continued to the next phone number on my list.

Speaking with a literary agent.
Thanks for returning my call.
Oh, I heard your call come in, but I screen my calls. Strike one.
I don't want to talk to half the people who call me. Strike two.

Strike one: I don't believe in screening calls that come into a business line. Since many people have their caller ID blocked, you can't assume that "blocked caller" is a sales call. You may even lose business to someone who answers his phone, because potential customers tend to call several people to find someone to hire, and they want help NOW. Strike two: Not wanting to talk to "half the people" sounds unfriendly. If and when he doesn't return my future call, I will assume that I am in that half. Then, I'll wonder why I'm in that half, and why he didn't have the courage to tell me so. If you are adamant about screening calls, don't tell people that you screen.

Speaking with a store cashier.

Do you have [x] magazine?

I don't know; check aisle three. Strike one.

I did.

It would be there.

I know, but I didn't see it there.

Then we don't have it.

Can I have help looking for it?

There isn't anyone here to help you look. Strike two.

He hollers about the magazine to another cashier who gives a look like "How should I know?" Strike three.

Can you look up the magazine in an inventory database?

The person who can help you with that left at five. Strike four.

So, you lose a lot of potential business after 5 p.m.

Call tomorrow. Strike five.

Strikes one and three: As I mentioned many times in this book, KNOW YOUR INVENTORY. Know what you have and be knowledgeable about each item. It's alright to have a cheat sheet/book/database. If you don't know something off the top of your head, then you should have the resources to look it up.

Strikes two and four: Having no one available to help me, during business hours, is one of the stupidest things that I've ever heard. How can that be? Why be open if you can't help your customers? This store simply has robots working during certain hours. Accordingly, more detailed operating hours should be posted in the store's window: **From 9 a.m.-5 p.m. we have people available to help you. After 5 p.m. don't bother asking us for help; our robotics team only knows how to run the cash registers.** Strike five: Why would I waste my time calling a store that isn't helpful? Remember that you must be able to make a sale when customers are ready, otherwise they will go somewhere else or lose interest.

Speaking with a computer company's field tech.
Thank you for your great work. I appreciate your help.
How do you like working for the company?
It's OK. It doesn't pay very well. Strike one.
I met the owner. He seems like a nice person.
He's OK. Strike two.

Strikes one and two: What do your employees say about you and your company? Having good employees isn't enough to stay in business. If they portray that they aren't treated well, customers will take their business elsewhere. I was tempted to tell the tech that I would hire him if he were to start his own business. He would have his first customer, and the other company would have one less customer. If you are playing the role of the tech, rather than the employer, you have an obligation to say positive things about your employer. If you can't say anything nice, then quit. In the meantime, say that the company is great and the boss is nice.

Speaking with the owner of a public relations firm.
Here's the payment. I look forward to everyone knowing about my book.
We'll get started right away.
The next morning I receive a fax that is a copy of my receipt of yesterday's payment. A handwritten note on the paper states that my money is being refunded, because he doesn't have time to help me. A bigger account came along. Strike one.
He didn't even have the courtesy or courage to call me.
I see him around town, but he never says, "Hello." Strike two.

Strike one: The owner of the company was right to refund my money, since he decided not to help me, but he made a commitment to work with me. If you decide that you can't help someone, you should part ways. Turning back on a commitment, because a bigger account came along, is terrible! What a great way to show someone that you don't value her project, investment, or feelings. He should have either told the other company that he can't start on his project right away, or hired someone to help him with the increased workload.
Strike two: No matter how badly customer relationships end, be cordial when you see them in the future. Say, "Hello." Don't give them more reasons to dislike your company. Even if disgruntled people were just potential customers, they deserve gratitude for considering hiring you. Be nice and they may contact you, again.

Speaking with a storage facility worker.

I am about to leave, but my storage unit's door won't close all the way.

The worker "speeds" toward me in a golf cart waving his finger and yelling at me from twenty yards away.

Move it [my truck] now! Strike one.

I wait for him to drive up to me.

Don't yell at me.

I told you to move your truck a half hour ago.

It wasn't that long.

I'm leaving, but I can't shut the door.

He storms over to my unit and shoves the lock into place. He yells at me one more time before he drives off.

Strike one: Where do I begin? Do I even have to spell it out? *Never* yell at a customer. This worker and his wife are such mean people that they supply me with pages and pages worth of vignettes suitable for this chapter. So, how is the business still alive? The weekend worker does a great job with damage control, plus the owner of this company has no idea what is happening at his facility. Well, at least he didn't until I wrote a letter. Why am I still a customer? I am writing a customer service manual, and I need material!

Speaking with a landscape architect.

I'm still upset, because I'm still finding cigarette buttes that your workers left behind—all over my new plants—and because I'm still finding a lot of nails in the mulch.

Well, you seem to be doing a good job picking them up.

Strike one.

What?!

He storms off to the other side of my property.

A few minutes later, he walks by me closely and stares me down.

Oh, so one minute you're happy and the next minute you decide you're still mad?! Strike two.

I immediately go into my house and lock the door.

Strike one: Instead of being sarcastic, the landscaper could have apologized and offered a solution. He also could have offered me a partial refund. I am a firm believer in refunds and credits when you don't do what you promised when you promised. The customer deserves a show of gratitude for her patience and aggravation.

Strike two: *Never* bully a customer—especially at one's home. The last thing you want to do is make customers feel unsafe and uneasy that you know where they live. If customers don't trust you, they will never hire you, again, or refer you to their friends.

Speaking with a rental truck company employee.

Hi, I'm Jeanne Murdock. I have a reservation.

Let's see. Oh, yes. Here you are. You have a reservation for today—the mid-size truck.

Yes, that's right.

Oh, we don't have any trucks available. Strike one.

But, I made a reservation.

We've had a lot of people needing trucks. Strike two.

Including me, and I made a reservation.

Well, I can't just make a truck appear. I wish I could. Then, I could supply everyone with a truck. Strike three.

I just drove 30 miles to get here. Why didn't you call me to tell me that I couldn't have a truck today?

You're not the only one who wants a truck. I can't call everyone. Strike four.

Just come back tomorrow.

Why do they have to be the only rental truck company in the county?

Strike one: *Always* deliver what you promised when you promised. No exceptions. No excuses.

Strike two: I don't care about the needs of the other customers. I don't want to be lumped in with the masses or treated like a number. He should have been honest and said, "I'm sorry. We overbooked." At least that statement, although another poor business practice, would have been the truth.

Strike three: Don't make stupid comments or jokes. Just be honest, admit your mistakes, and succinctly look for an immediate solution.

Strike four: Ah! I wasn't the only customer to whom this happened. He let down several other people. Put your customers' needs before your own. By the way, overbooking, for which airlines are notorious, is a practice under the assumption that some customers will flake (cancel without notification). But if not enough customers flake, then *you* become the flake—the one who doesn't fulfill a promise. It is better to have vacancies than angry customers.

Speaking with a business owner.

I hope that I can make it to the front door without the owner seeing me. He hates me. He'll probably be pissed to see me here.

Hi. Bye.

Damn. He saw me.

Jeanne, hold on. I want to talk to you.

Yes.

What are you doing here?

I explain, but he doesn't seem to understand how much I help his business and his customers.

One of your employees asked me to come in.

He stands up and his face turns dark red and his body shakes from rage.

He puts his hands on his hips.

Don't you ever come in here, again.

And I'm supposed to be afraid of him?! Ha! Laughable. His narcissism is about to make his head explode.

He chastises me. Strike one.

I cut him off after a minute.

OK. Bye.

Strike one: Unless a colleague or customer enters your company with the intention of hurting you or others, there is no reason to be rude. And, *never* bully a customer. If you have that much disdain for someone, just say, "I appreciate how you supported my company in the past, but it would be best if we part ways now. Please don't come into the store anymore. I hope that you can find someone better to fulfill your needs." Being polite and respectful goes a long way. Sandwiching the bad news is very effective, too. As you can read from the above quote, I said something nice before and after the request to terminate the relationship.

Speaking with a retirement home resident.
He witnesses the resident director treating me poorly.
I'm sorry.
It's not your fault.
I'm sorry. Strike one.
You don't have to apologize for how he's acting.
He's really stressed about everything that's going on
around here. Strike two.
Then, he's working the wrong job.

Strike one: You know your behavior is really bad if one of
your customers has to apologize for you. It also means that
you don't possess compassion to apologize for yourself.
The resident director also overlooked how fortunate he was
to have such a nice resident—a source right there for him to
learn compassion. Don't let yourself become so stressed
that your focus switches from the needs of your customers
to your own agenda. Stop. Take a breath. Remove the
blinders and look around.
Strike two: Even worse than a customer apologizing for
your behavior is one making excuses for your behavior. It
doesn't matter what is going on in your personal life or
business life; it is *never* acceptable to treat a customer
poorly. Whatever is bothering you, leave your (emotional)
baggage at the door. Then, walk into your office or store
with a clear mind and desire to help others.

Speaking with a store cashier.
There's silence until my items are rung up.
That'll be $45.87.
You forgot to say, "Hello."
Oh, I'm sorry. I forgot. I'm terrible at remembering
"Hello" and "Goodbye." Strike one.
Then, you're in the wrong career.
I'm good at everything in between.

Strike one: Even though the cashier was in the wrong
career, he was a sweet kid. Maybe he could work hard to
remember greetings and salutations—he would have to in
order to provide good customer service. Customers want to
be acknowledged, appreciated, and thanked for their
patronage. They want a reason to return, besides filling a
need or want. Ringing up groceries, cashiers can view each
product as just a number, but customers can't be treated
that way.

Speaking with a rental truck company agent.

I rent a truck and collect the key on a Saturday, but don't use the truck until Sunday when the office is closed. I return Monday to issue my complaint.

I showed up, yesterday, to pick up the truck, but it wasn't on the street like you promised.

Oh, I forgot. Strike one.

I was frantic, because I didn't think that my mover could get the truck out of your yard, since another truck was blocking it.

Well, you got it out, right? Strike two.

Yes, but while I was waiting for the mover to meet me here I was stressed, because that was the only day that I had to move. You can imagine the implications, can't you?

Well, you got the truck out.

Yes, but if I hadn't been able to get the truck out, I would have lost hundreds of dollars and been in a huge bind.

Well, you shouldn't have taken the key Saturday.

What do you mean?

How could I put the truck on the street for you if you took the key? Strike three.

Don't you have a spare?

No.

I called your after-hours number, but it sounded like some sex line.

What?

It turns out that there is a typo—the phone number on the door is wrong by one digit. Strike four.

Strike one: Always do what you say you're going to do, when you say you're going to do it. Write yourself a note, so that you never have to say, "I forgot."

Strike two: When a customer is upset, listen. The agent kept skirting my concern. I needed him to acknowledge my predicament and apologize for creating a stressful situation. This dialogue would have made me feel heard and understood: "It sounds like my forgetfulness almost put you in a real bind. You must have been really stressed and worried. I'm sorry that my actions created a burden for you. What can I do to make it up?"

Strike three: Always accept responsibility when you do something wrong—never put it back on the customer. Save the deflection shield for when you're sunbathing. Or, is that a reflection shield? Anyway.

Strike four: If you can't get your phone number right, then you don't deserve to be in business. Step aside, and let the rest of us thrive.

Speaking with an airline representative.
Need I say more? I will anyway.
I'm calling to tell you that I won't be on the first leg of my reserved flight.
OK It will be $150 to change your reservation.
I'm not changing it; I'm just not going to be on the first leg.
That's a change and a charge of $150.
I was told that if I'm not going to be on the first leg, I have to tell you, otherwise you won't let me on the second leg. I was also told there wouldn't be a fee.
You were told wrong. Strike one.

Strike one: First, you must assume that the customer is telling the truth. Second, if you're a part of a multi-million-dollar company, be pliable. Bend the rules a little to satisfy a customer—especially if one of your employees made a mistake. I believe that it is important to be consistent with policies, particularly from customer to customer, but be willing to make exceptions. Your number one concern is that you retain your current customers and keep them satisfied.

Speaking with a store clerk.

Hi. Tell me about the event you're having today.

He starts explaining.

Then, his manager rushes up to him and interrupts the conversation that the clerk and I are having. Strike one. The manager says something that doesn't sound like an emergency and then walks away.

A few minutes later, the clerk and I are still talking, and the manager walks up to the clerk and moves him aside to reach for a piece of paper. Strike two.

Gosh, he's rude.

It's OK. He's the boss.

Strikes one and two: Don't interrupt. It makes me so mad to wait five minutes, patiently, to speak with someone, and then someone else barrels in to capitalize the first person's attention. Wait your damn turn! Regarding the above scenario, what is more important than a clerk helping a customer and closing the deal? The manager should have waited to speak with his clerk. He clearly was an impolite person who treated his clerk and customer with disrespect. He even had his employee brainwashed to think that his status made such poor treatment acceptable. If you find yourself in a similar situation where you're the clerk, take the manager aside and express that you don't appreciate being interrupted or pushed.

Speaking with a furniture store employee.
Hi. I saw your sign that states, "Going out of business sale." I'm sorry that you'll be closing. When is your last day?
Oh, we're not closing.
Really?
Oh, no. That's just the type of sale we have right now.
So, you're not closing?
No, we're just trying to get more customers. Strike one.

Strike one: It is much more effective to get new customers by sending the message that business is booming. Why not have a "Business is booming sale"? "We're slashing prices, because we can afford to, thanks to your patronage." If business is slow or you portray that you are closing your doors, people will assume that it is because you offer poor customer service or that you don't have a good product, for example. Also, having a going out of business sale without going out of business is deceiving and depletes public trust. One would wonder what else you're hiding.

Speaking with a store cashier.
There's silence until my items are rung up.
That'll be $10.19.
You forgot to say, "Hello."
You didn't say, "Hello," either. Strike one.
I'm not the one providing customer service.
He slams my food down at the end of the counter and walks away in a huff.

Strike one: Always greet your customers, acknowledge them, and show that you are happy to see them. In the past, some cashiers have told me that they forgot to say, "Hello," which I don't understand, but I let it slide if they apologize and proceed to be genuinely nice. In the case above, the cashier had no intention of being nice and resented my pointing it out. If you're always grumpy, don't get a job where you work directly with customers. If you're grumpy sometimes, either don't go to work that day, or leave your baggage at the door.

Speaking with a hotel clerk.
Hi, did you hear the fire alarm going off?
No. Strike one.
It was going off in my room.
Oh.
It was going off for about 30 minutes.
Was there a fire?
No, there was too much steam from my shower.
Oh.
Why didn't anyone come to my room when the alarm sounded?
Was there a fire?
No.
We continue to talk in circles.

Strike one: What good is a fire alarm in your business if no action is taken when it sounds? Since fire alarms are for the safety of your business, customers, and employees, people feel safe knowing that the alarms are installed and functional. I didn't feel safe when my alarm sounded and no one responded. What if something else bad happened and I needed emergency assistance? Would anyone respond? Make sure that you have your emergency action plans in place, up to date, and rehearsed.

Speaking with an off-airport parking lot manager.

I'm wondering why I was charged an extra $5.

It's a service fee.

Service fee? I already paid you $9 per day.

Yes, but we had to shuttle you to and from the airport. Gas is expensive. We only charge $5, and some other lots charge twice that. **Strike one.**

I didn't see anywhere on your website or in your lot that you charge an extra $5.

Oh, it's on the website.

No, it's not. I read the whole thing thoroughly.

Well, it's at the end if you pay online.

I didn't pay online.

Well all of our customers know that we charge an extra $5. Strike two.

So, you're punishing first-time customers and those who don't pay in advance?

We're not punishing you, ma'am.

Strike one: How do you define fraud? I define it by reading a parking lot website that states in big letters: FREE SHUTTLE and then hides the shuttle fee in the "service fee." It's alright to figure various costs into one fee, but you can't say that something is free and then charge for it. Strike two: Even if the service fee were rational, the business owner didn't make sure that all of his customers had the same information. This point is crucial. Make sure that you include everyone in your disclosure of policies, fees, and procedures.

Speaking with a waiter.

Can I please have tea?

He brings me the tea. I start eating the food that I brought in with me, because the restaurant doesn't cater to the gluten-free diet that I have to follow.

The waiter returns a minute later.

You can't eat your food in here. Strike one.

I can't eat your food.

It's against the law. If something goes wrong with your food, we could be liable. Strike two.

What could happen? Uh Oh. My food could actually make me healthy?! If they're worried about liability, maybe they shouldn't serve fried food or allow smoking.

I am kicked to the curb—literally—for eating my own food. Here I sit, beside the cigarettes, eating my gluten-free meal and drinking the beverage I just bought. Now I can check "demeaning experience" off my bucket list. I'm losing my appetite for the only food that keeps me alive.

Strike one: The waiter was so intrusive. He could have said, "Hi. I notice that you're eating food that you brought in. Can I get you something from our menu?"

Strike two: I'm told that it's not proper to ask for sympathy, but everyone needs it every once in awhile. After I said that I couldn't eat the restaurant's food, the waiter could have shown sympathy and asked for more information. Instead, he gave me the reason why I couldn't eat my food in there, even though I didn't ask why. Remember, don't give reasons for your policies, unless you're asked, and only then say, "That's just what works best for our company." By that time, do you really think that I cared to hear legal jargon? I actually went back into the restaurant, after I was done eating, to finish listening to a band. Unfortunately, the waiter missed his opportunity to apologize and say something like, "I'm so sorry about what happened. I didn't mean for you to leave and eat on the curb. I would have really liked to have found something that you could eat. What can I do to make it up?"

Speaking with a gas station owner.

I can't find any paper towels, water, or squeegees. Don't you have any? Strike one.

Without facial expression or words, he vaguely looks around the store. Then, he grabs napkins and hands them to me.

Napkins?! I can't work on my car with napkins. The most I can do with napkins is wipe the grease off my face.

OK. And don't you have any water and squeegees?

He shakes his head. Then, he points toward the door.

He motioned for me to grab a bucket that contained water and a squeegee.

Alright. So, are you going to carry it out for me?

No. You take it and bring it back. *Now* he speaks. Strike two.

I'll take it and then you can come get it.

Strike one: Long gone are the days when we could count on an attendant to walk out to our car to help us at a gas station. If a gas station owner expects his customers to be independent, he has to provide the resources for such. A gas station owner who doesn't provide paper towels is a tight wad. If I have to pay as much as I do for gas, then I want some damn paper towels. Offering amenities at a gas station improves the customer service experience, which is key for retaining customers. Listen to your customers; they'll tell you what they need to make their life a little bit easier. Simplify their life and you'll have a long-time customer.

Strike two: This business owner didn't have anything to say until he told me to do what he should have done for me. He should have said, "Let me take that outside for you. On the way, I will get you clean water. I'm so sorry for the inconvenience. Thank you for your feedback. You're right. I really should have everything by the pump for you and my other valued customers. Rest assured that I will

have everything you need by the next time you're here."
Am I living in a fantasy expecting that quote? Well, The
Successful—highlighted in Chapter 1—talk like that.

Speaking with a store employee.
Could I please have change for the parking meter?
Sorry, we don't have enough change. Strike one.

Strike one: If your store is located on a street with parking
meters, you better have a vault full of quarters. How can
you expect customers if they have nowhere to park? Give
change bountifully. More time on the meter equates more
time in your store. More time in your store equates more
money spent. Also, providing change is an example of
going beyond your normal customer service duties. Even if
someone doesn't need to patronize your store that day,
they'll remember that you were accommodating and that
you will likely provide great customer service in the future.
In the above vignette, since the store employee didn't help
me, I had to go somewhere else to get change, a store
where I subsequently bought something.

Sitting at a restaurant.

I'm freezing! Why do they have to blast the air conditioning? I guess they don't want people to linger after eating.

The waiter doesn't acknowledge that I'm bent over the table hugging myself and rocking. Strike one.

Strike one: It always amazes me when employees in many businesses ignore my obvious discomfort, whether it's because the building is too cold, too smelly, or too loud, for example. They just go on with their routine because they're comfortable. I have found that waiters are notorious for wanting the restaurant cool, because they're running around for several hours. But, they have to remember, if they don't create a nice ambiance for the customers, the customers won't return. No customers, no job. I see this situation on planes, too. The passengers are all grabbing blankets and jackets and the stewardesses don't change the cabin temperature.

Give customers your full and undivided attention and listen to what they say. They'll tell you what they need. Be patient, courteous, and non-confrontational.

I hope that the above vignettes helped. If you could identify with any of the professionals, then it is time either to change careers or follow my suggestions. All is not hopeless unless you don't care about people in general. If that's the case, then maybe you should work with animals.

CHAPTER 4

TEN LAMEST EXCUSES FOR NOT RETURNING A PHONE CALL

1. I've been really busy.

Me, too. You know why? Because I have to spend so much time re-calling people who don't return my phone calls. Everyone has the same hours in the day. Assume that everyone is as busy as you. The bottom line is that you should respect everyone's time and situation as much as you do your own. What does your outgoing message say? "I'll call you back when I return to the office." Do you? "I will return your call as soon as possible." Do you? Define soon. "I'll call you back within 24 hours." Do you? Make a point to return all calls within 24 hours. If you can't keep up, hire help. Everyone deserves an immediate response. If you subscribe to the thinking, "Well, if it were important he'll call back," then you're doomed.

2. I was out of the country.

When you know that you will be out of the office for more than a day, change your outgoing message to reflect such. "I am out of the office and will be returning _____." It also helps to offer an alternative person in your office (and phone number) who can help customers.

3. I was out sick for a week.

But, I called you and left a message a month ago. What happened the other three weeks? Let me guess. You had to play catch up when you returned to the office and decided that I wasn't important enough to call. Again, make accommodations when you know that you will be out of the office, so that colleagues and customers aren't left hanging. If you're home when you realize that you can't make it into the office, either have your calls forwarded to your home or to another person at your work. Learn to control your work phone remotely or have someone at the office do it for you.

4. I'm much better by email.

That doesn't say much if you suck at email, also. When it comes to customer satisfaction, communicate with each person the way each person prefers. As far as mass communications, I understand why you would only choose one way. For all other correspondence, ask each person how she wants to keep in touch and then accommodate accordingly.

5. I couldn't find your phone number.

It's annoying how unresourceful people are. My phone number is on my business card, newsletter, email signature, website, your answering machine, and caller ID. Do a lot of leg work to track down a customer. If you have to, email the customer or write to her home address. Try contacting a customer who is friends with the other customer. Walk to the end of the earth to find the customer's phone number. If you don't, then you can blame your disorganization for having one fewer customer.

6. My phone broke.

Make sure to have a back-up system for your phone. And back-ups for your back-ups. I'm assuming that my phone number was in your phone. Again, use other resources to find a customer's phone number. Or, maybe the issue is that you have the customer's phone number, but you're not willing to borrow a phone to call her. If you don't show that you are willing to make an effort with a customer and even go out of your comfort zone, then she will feel unimportant. Consequently, you will lose that customer.

7. I don't have the information (or answer) you requested.

You need to do what you say you're going to do when you said you would do it—100% of the time. If you promise to call a customer on Wednesday with information requested, and you neither call nor have the information, then you get two strikes. To get only one strike, call on Wednesday and say, "I said that I would have the information for you, today, but I need more time. I will call you either way in two more days." It is really important not to leave a customer waiting. If a customer finds you unreliable, then she will "go to the fish store down the street."

8. I had a family emergency.

Family emergency seems to be redundant, doesn't it? By definition, there will regularly be something pressing that arises in your family. When my mom died unexpectedly, I gave myself an hour to get ready to drive three hours to be with my family. Before I left home, I gathered everything I needed for a week's worth of work. To wrap up her affairs, I made the journey several more times during a six-month period, bringing my work along with me. I was so organized and respectful of my clients and colleagues that 99% of the people in my work life didn't even know that I had a death in the family. I also believe in keeping my personal life separate from my business life. Anyway, if you can't take calls, change your outgoing message to reflect when you will be able to return calls.

9. I thought that I would run into you.

It's so nice to be able to communicate with people in person, rather than on the phone, let alone email. Unfortunately, you can't rely on seeing a customer around town or in your business. Be sure to return each call within 24 hours. Returning calls should be a high priority; think of it as job security.

10. I asked _____ to call you.

How do I know that you asked a colleague to call me if you don't tell me? If you pass the buck, tell the customer. You can either return the customer's call or copy her on an email to inform her that you asked someone else to help her. Either way, tell her the name of the person who will call her, his phone number, and when he will call.

CONCLUSION

Two of the characteristics I found each of The Successful to possess are patience and compassion. Other factors necessary for treating customers well include liking (preferably loving) your job, caring about the success of the business, leaving your baggage at the door, not over committing, listening (Shhh! Listen!), being organized, accepting customer suggestions, and establishing trust.

If you are on the verge of going out of business, take a long retrospective look at how you treated customers, before you blame your demise on the economy. If you have customer feedback forms, read those, or ask customers to fill out a confidential survey. You may be able to salvage your business and even create a boon if you overhaul your service using the tips in this book.

I'd like to sum up this book by answering the age-old question: Is the customer always right? What do you think? Really. How do you answer this question and what is your reasoning? I believe that the customer is definitely *not* always right, but you should make her think that she is.

OTHER READING

Hopkins, T. *How to Master the Art of Selling.* Warner Books. 1982.

Nathan, R, Stuart, M. *Coping with the Stressed-Out People in Your Life.* Ballantine Books. 1994.

Navarro, J, Karlins, M. *What Every Body is Saying: An Ex-FBI Agent's Guide to Speed Reading People.* William Morrow Paperbacks. 2008.

Tracy, B. *Thinking Big: The Keys to Personal Power and Maximum Performance.* Simon & Schuster Audio/Nightingale-Conant. 2007.

ABOUT THE AUTHOR

Jeanne "Bean" Murdock is a satirist and business consultant who fuses humor with customer service education. When she is not teaching customer service, she writes and edits for other businesses to help them be memorable.

Originally from Cupertino, CA, Jeanne studied physical education at California Polytechnic State University in San Luis Obispo, and then started BEANFIT Health and Fitness Services in 1992. Three years later, she was diagnosed with celiac disease. For the first 12 years in business, Jeanne focused on personal fitness training and nutrition counseling.

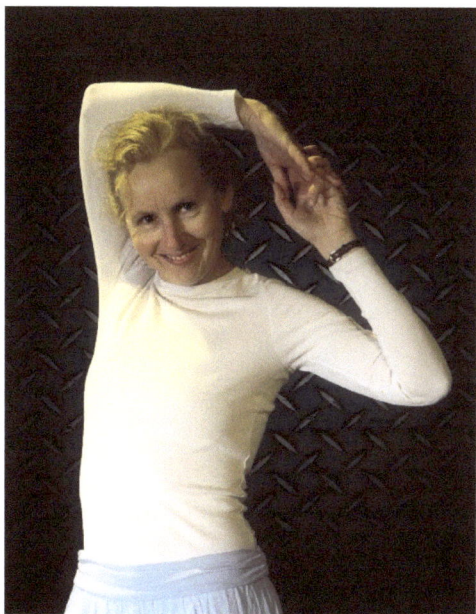

Image by Jim Tyler, edited by Greg Heller

Qualifications:

--Bachelor of Science in Physical Education
concentration in Commercial/Corporate Fitness
Cal Poly State University, San Luis Obispo.

--Undergraduate Nutrition Coursework Completed
San Diego State University.

Questions? Comments? Please feel free to write or call Jeanne "Bean" Murdock anytime at:

P.0. Box 1083
Paso Robles, CA 93447
Phone: 408-203-7643
Website: www.JeanneMurdock.com
E-mail: info@jeannemurdock.com

Visit www.JeanneMurdock.com for other products by
Jeanne Murdock, including:
*The Every Excuse in the Book Book: How to Benefit from
Exercising, by Overcoming Your Excuses* and
*Successful Dating at Last! A Workbook for Understanding
Each Other*